Trouble Can Be So Beautiful at the Beginning

The poems in *Trouble Can Be So Beautiful at the Beginning* are more than poems. They are old photos in a family album, handwritten recipes in a tin box. In this beautiful collection, Shuly Xóchitl Cawood examines what it means to be human—the places that hold us, the people we lose. Each poem, its "small, still words a sigh / of ink," helps us recognize who we are and remember who we used to be. Cawood's words are "soft as water / stronger than an undertow." Her poems are time machines, love letters. Maps marked up with stars.

—Melissa Fite Johnson, author of *Green*

Shuly Xóchitl Cawood's collection, *Trouble Can Be So Beautiful at the Beginning*, opens with: "The way he leans in and says, *I promise,* / his copper eyes like pennies / you have plenty of…" and you find yourself leaning in, wanting more. From there you tumble into a rich and vibrant world, one that stretches from Ohio to Mexico, from "the east coast / and west coast of our bed," from family to friendship to love to loss and back again, from one emotion to another: "rotten then revived, start drowning but burst / above surface for air." This collection pulls the reader along until the very last poem.

—Courtney LeBlanc, author of *Beautiful & Full of Monsters*

Shuly Xóchitl Cawood's poems shine with love and authenticity. They take us from the cornfields of Ohio to her ancestral home in Mexico. The trouble that she finds there IS beautiful—"a flame tilting like curiosity." She thinks "about what it means to follow someone to the edge of nothing." She wonders if she can learn to live with emptiness. Throughout this journey there are promises, doubts, unspoken fears, but there is always an undertow nudging her toward home, toward her *abuelitos*, and her *tia*'s kitchen where words, food, and laughter co-mingle like the swirl of incense and prayer.

—Cathryn Essinger, author of *The Apricot and the Moon*

I0809352

Winner of the Adrienne Bond Poetry Award

Previous Winners

Seaborn Jones, *Going Farther into the Woods than the Woods Go*
(published 2012)

Kelly Whiddon, *The House Began to Pitch*
(published 2013)

Megan Sexton, *Swift Hour*
(published 2014)

Philip Lee Williams, *The Color of All Things: 99 Love Poems*
(published 2015)

Lesley Dauer, *Carnival Life*
(published 2016)

Katy Giebenhain, *Sharps Cabaret*
(published 2017)

Sara Pirkle Hughes, *The Disappearing Act*
(published 2018)

R. T. Smith, *Summoning Shades*
(published 2019)

William Woolfitt, *Spring Up Everlasting*
(published 2020)

Trouble Can Be So Beautiful at the Beginning

POEMS

Shuly Xóchitl Cawood

MERCER UNIVERSITY PRESS
Macon, Georgia
2021

MUP/ P616

Published by Mercer University Press
1501 Mercer University Drive
Macon, Georgia 31207

25 24 23 22 21 5 4 3 2 1

Books published by Mercer University Press are printed on acid-free paper that meets the requirements of the American National Standard for Information Sciences—Permanence of Paper for Printed Library Materials.

Printed and bound in the United States.

This book is set in Adobe Garamond Pro.

Cover/jacket design by Burt&Burt.

Library of Congress Cataloging-in-Publication Data

Names: Cawood, Shuly Xóchitl, author.
Title: Trouble can be so beautiful at the beginning / Shuly Xóchitl Cawood.
Description: Macon, Georgia : Mercer University Press, 2021. | Winner of the Adrienne Bond Poetry Award. |
Identifiers: LCCN 2020050988 | ISBN 9780881467765 (paperback)
Subjects: LCGFT: Poetry.
Classification: LCC PS3603.A975 T76 2021 | DDC 811/.6--dc23
LC record available at https://lccn.loc.gov/2020050988

To Imogene Bolls and David Citino,
then and now

Several of the poems in this collection have been individually published—some in different versions and with different titles—in the following places, and I gratefully acknowledge them here:

"Aguascalientes, 1919," *Cider Press Review*, 2017

"After She Calls and Says She Wants You Back," *Harbor Review,* 2018

"After the Diagnosis," *Qu*, 2019

"Cooking," *Rust+Moth,* 2016

"Designed by Fire," *Queen of Cups,* 2017

"Escape," *Helix Magazine*, 2013

"Finding Alicia" (now "Less"), *Moving Out,* 1995

"Grand Theft," *december magazine*, 2018

"If," *Plainsongs*, 2019

"Immigrant," *Lunch Ticket,* 2018

"Inheritance," *The Sun*, 2020

"Katy Perry Is Crooning and Won't Stop Just Because I Did," *Brevity*, 2018

"Like Love," *New Southern Fugitives*, 2018

"Lovers," *The Independent Weekly,* 2001

"Mother," *The Pegasus Review,* 1995

"On Sundays," *december magazine*, 2018

"Present Tense," *Label Me Latina/o,* 2015

"Puerto Escondido, Mexico," *Change Seven,* 2015

"Roots," *JuxtaProse Literary Magazine*, 2018

"Savior," *Prime Number Magazine,* 2017

"Secret Ingredient," *Santa Clara Review*, 2018

"The Day After Getting Back the Medical Test Results,"
Change Seven, 2015

"This Foreign Place," *San Pedro River Review,* 2016

"This Way Home," *wildness,* 2017

"Tormenta de Tierra," *Naugatuck River Review,* 2013

"Trouble Can Be So Beautiful at the Beginning,"
Glass: A Journal of Poetry, 2018

"What Mickey Wants," *Change Seven,* 2015

MERCER
UNIVERSITY

MERCER UNIVERSITY PRESS

Endowed by

TOM WATSON BROWN
and
THE WATSON-BROWN FOUNDATION, INC.

Contents

Trouble Can Be So Beautiful at the Beginning

Trouble Can Be So Beautiful at the Beginning

Yellow ruffles of dandelion, so much like crêpe
paper, so open its flower face.

A struck match, the flame tilting like curiosity.

The forest that beckons you deep into its pine,
needles soft in your palm,
the way the path skinnies like it knows
exactly where it is going.

The way he leans in and says, *I promise,*
his copper eyes like pennies
you have plenty of, that you don't think
one day it will be so hard to lose.

Roots

No one knows where my *abuelito* was born, from which woman
he burst forth, in what city or village or windowless room,
in what hot and hurried season.

What I know is this: my *abuelito* liked his feet rubbed
with mud-thick lotion, and he ordered his daughters
to look up crossword puzzle words—spellings and origins—
and he begot a set of sons with someone else,
before he married my stricter *abuelita.* He chose
my Tío Juan's name even though my grandmother
had selected an elegant other, even though
she had specifically told my *abuelito*
no, no, no when it came to names like Juan—
so common it might slip by unnoticed.

Perhaps my grandfather wanted no one else
to be remarkable but instead to disappear
as he did after work at the railway company,
after dinner, after his necessary *carne, tortillas, frijoles,*
back into the city streets so that he might sit somewhere dark
and shake the last *hielo* in his glass as if it were the roll of dice,
so that he might become someone else or do God knows what.

What I want is his real name, and from whom he stole the one he wore
and with what other truths he gambled and for what price.
I would like to know if he wept the night they brought a bowl
of bloody water from my grandmother's bedroom—another son,
finally, after so many daughters—yet no one ever spoke
about this one, two hours old, and he would never have a name
I might hold onto all these decades later. Maybe my *abuelito*
did not want to name him, or named him but swallowed it
like so many other secrets, dark and bitter and better
left dead.

Aguascalientes, 1919

Who remembers her now with her polka-dotted dress, without sleeves, without any reason why she couldn't say no when you asked to drive her home from the dance? You did not even like to dance, but there were so many other reasons to go: the softened, wooden floor gave just enough, the music swelled and slowed, and her strap fell at just the right moment.

In this city you could make anyone believe you danced, even the girl with polka dots, the girl you eyed all night with her best friend, Lucita, who frowned in your direction. Lucita had no chance against this cobalt sky, this moon you cut yourself with a silver pocket knife. You gave the girl without sleeves, *sin mangas*, your name against the cold, and she took it, such open hands waiting for more, the same way she held them wide open later that night in the back seat of the car you borrowed without asking, the way you did everything, promising you would bring it back just the way you found it.

Lovers

When we visit my *tía*,
my aunt in Torreón,
I sleep in the house,
the garden like a green moat
around white stucco walls.

She gives me a king-size bed,
and I doze off on one side and awaken
on the other of this gold-comforter

island.

Beyond the lemon tree and yard,
he sleeps in a twin bed with two blankets
in the room off the garage where she sews,

her measuring tapes like yellow snakes,
and her laces, chiffons, silks
bundled on the table and every bit of chair.
She's cleared a space
on just one shelf
for his bag.

He awakens to the swish
of her old bridal dress
hanging loose and thin
from a black wire hanger,
its sleeves dusting walls
in the breeze.

Like Love

In memoriam: Anton Yelchin, 1989-2016

There's no telling at the beginning what this will lead to.
You shake hands, you make a pact with yourself you are brand new.
You roll down the windows of this new love, let the salt of ocean
air reach you and don't worry about rust. Not yet, anyway.

There will be trips into the canyon and out, and up the highway
to towns that don't recognize you, that teach you to be open,
to cities with lungs of flashing lights and traffic stops and car
crashes that remind you to breathe this existence like it's never
gonna leave you. You press the gas pedal and rise from vale
to hill, born anew wild into the future. This love, ring
and pinions, engine and steel.

You don't yet know what makes you feel powerful
can also crush you, or you know it but never imagine it,
not like the way it will happen, the moment calm,
a standstill—the kind that allows you to glance away,
that lets your mind wander for a moment so you don't
see it coming. It'll shift fast like the punch of a fist
and pin you to the next moment and the next

until the beginning—Leningrad not yet Saint Petersburg,
the continent of your life still vast and complicated—
slips from this place, easy and willing, this breath, this broken-
open heart.

Let's Move

Before Michelle Obama and long before
her campaign about childhood obesity,
back in 1940, someone snapped a photo
of my father on his first birthday
sitting on the front lawn of the house
on Ivy Hill. It is cold on this November day
in Kentucky's coal country, but there he is
bundled in coat and hat and boots
and he's a chubby baby, quite a roly-poly—
this, my grandmother's doing—and before him
also sits a fat birthday cake nearly his size,
slathered in frosting, and from the looks
of the picture, dessert will all be his.

Long before Michelle Obama and her husband's
presidential campaign, decades before Rosa Parks
and Brown versus Board of Education, two years
before giving birth to my father, my grandmother
believed in separate not equal. She also lost
a nine-month-old son. These two things, unrelated,
except to say: fear eclipses reason and imagination.

Perhaps my grandmother stuffed my father
with all the hope she could muster in her kitchen
cupboards, with whatever she could bake
and ice and sweeten because in 1940
she could not imagine he might live longer than a year
just as she could not fathom a Barack Obama
with his yellow-dressed and beautiful wife,
his hand on the Bible, the other raised high.

Less

We have always wanted less
and we whittle ourselves
to small notches
of knuckle
and elbow.

I understand how you tug
into smaller jeans,
nibble at crackers,
shrink your wrists and waist
with every meal you do not eat.

I have been there:
calorie countdowns,
all the crazy numbers,
the agony of a wished-for
wafer of self. The terror
of an extra ounce.
When I was just fifteen

I saw beauty in the way
my middle bridged, each rib
a thin, defatted plank.

My mother took a photo of the bone-child
I'd become. But, oh, we have
such mirrors no one else
can ever know.

This Foreign Place

I. Reuniting after one month apart

The sun glazes the wet street,
runs along the curb with us to Xola,
where VW Bugs and wheezing mint-colored buses splash
through bits of trash
and branches.

We're alone
among pressed uniforms
of giggling Mexican schoolchildren
and old women shuffling down the road
each with a brown scarf
fluttering around her head,
a flock of small sparrows.

My aunts and cousins remained
in their home, cooking stew
and playing cards
so we could hold hands
alone
on this *avenida.*

I wonder what will become of us later
when the street we are on is merely
plain and honest
not like Xola today
with its sooty air kicking
discarded newspapers,
making them flap,
which to us
sounds just
like applause.

II. Fear

In Oaxaca we lace up our shoes
and jog on streets with clapboard houses
and laundry lines with white garments, towels
that look like rows of jagged teeth.

The sun pants on us.

A mangy mutt lunges at me,
and you instantly yank my arm
and pull me back
behind you.
It is your arm
or leg in peril, possibly chewed.

This love, so new.

We sweat as we slowly
walk back to our room.

Sun licks our shoulders.

III. On the edge

Your hand moves onto my back
as if it were a canoe gliding
back and forth between neck
and tailbone.
You're trying to rub away my fever,
make me certain again
of where I am—

Taxco,
clinging
to a cliffside.

IV. Apart for the afternoon

Even as my skirt swishes
as if it were shaking its head,
bandits whistle, call out *bonita!*
and make me look straight ahead
so I cannot turn and see
yellow stucco churches
or woven mats waving
red and blue goodbyes
as I hurry, trying to find

that place
we promised
to return to.

I find you on a bench
the green color of a crocodile,
a blind man with a wooden cane
beside you. You do not see me—
the sun glares in your eyes,
falls on your coal-colored hair,
your mouth,
as if you were drowning in white.

For a moment
in another country

you look for me, unsure
if I will emerge
onto the plaza
through all that blaze
of light.

Mother

My *abuelita* cried the last time
my mother left her waving,
holding onto her black iron gate,
her Mexican home aqua
like ocean behind her.

Her last visit, my mother dragged
a mattress down the flight
of stairs to sleep by Abuelita's
bed, moved now into the dark dining room.
My grandmother didn't want
to hold a cane or walker,
so she held my mother's hand.

When my *abuelita* died
it was summer, and August raged
Ohio with ragweed.
Humidity clung like gauze.

My mother sat on our porch a long while.

Sometimes, she says, she still
feels her mother's hand in hers,
soft as water,

stronger than an undertow.

Good

My cousin, my *primo*, tells me let's go for a ride, opens
his truck door. He does not tell me where we are going,
and it does not matter. It is day or night or sometime in between
when dusk mingles light with dark, marries what we know
with what we don't.

My cousin has a beautiful face and a smile that could claim any heart.
He works on a ranch with long and sturdy fences, and he strides
within them wearing jeans and boots, and he manages cattle and feed
and numbers he does not try to explain to me. He leads a busy life
with a wife, a new baby, so many long hours keeping the ranch rich
with certainties.

My cousin shuts my door, shuts his, too, starts up the truck's bold
and thundering engine, flicks on the radio, pulls out onto the streets
of this city in Mexico, his home that he knows, that I do not. Not yet
anyway. I will teach in this place for the next four months,
and I will come to know what it expects

as we drive past the park a kilometer or two from my *tía's* house.
My *primo* points to landmarks, tries to show me the way. He uses
English so I will understand. I am twenty-four years old but
by the time I leave Mexico I will be twenty-five and I will know
enough Spanish, the color of its nuances, the shape of its many
meanings, not to translate in my head. But on this ride, I am still

twenty-four, and he is talking to me about American girls—as if
trying to assess if I am really one of them—and their reputation
to give it up easily, how it would be advised if I did not,
not just easily
but at all.

The streets loom strange through the windshield,
blurred and serpentine.

American girls give it up easily, and though later I will understand
I did not have to, in this cab of his truck, I hand over the words:
I've never done *it* before, I tell him. My mouth is as dry
as a communion wafer.

Good, he says or doesn't say.
Good.

I will be the only woman who runs alone around the park
a kilometer or two from my *tía's* house. Day after day, month
after month. The men will run in packs. I will be the only
woman who wears shorts instead of pants or sweats
when the temperatures flare. My American legs, bare and strong,

will take me round and round that park
past the men
until I find my way
until I am home
again.

Present Tense

My student, Elenita, won't learn
the English past tense.
She winds her lipsticked mouth
around words, chews the verb ends
into peppermint gum.
She shakes off the "ed" as easily
as she tosses her auburn hair.

For her it's a tense of failure:
tried, wanted, wasn't.
I frown and shake my head;
she shrugs with eyelash flutter.

She slinks
into my English
language class
in tight shirts,
hips snug in jeans,
hair pressed straight, in place.

She slides into Fernando's crook of arm
and giggles into his eyes.

She is present and perfect
this Torreón spring
as she saunters from class
with Fernando clutching
her books.

She leans into the flap of his black shirt
and they disappear into yellow desert sky.

Tonight I will read her essay,
the small, still words a sigh
of ink—

nothing to shove the crook
of Fernando's arm open

like the latch on a gate
giving way.

The Student

The president of my university, and some faculty, decided one day
to start up a magazine, except the magazine would have virtually
the same name as our student-run magazine. They told us
we had to change ours, never asked us politely, or ahead of time,
just said *you will change yours* only after it was a done deal.
At the time, I wasted many hours agonizing over what to do,
for I was full then of rules to abide by, and this was one: to do
as I was told, especially when the ones telling had the power
to expel.

Yet I was also full of wonder anyone could be that rude,
could disrespect the lot of us who sat on my living room floor
every week, poring over poems trying to make a lasting art
or at least have some part of ourselves endure even if we did not,
even though we would surely not. I decided, or we decided, not
to give in. We were keeping the name, we declared,
puffed up with courage.

The lesson, I thought then, was about strength and pride,
about standing up for myself, something I would do again
when I left the job that overworked and underpaid me,
when I left the man who loved but overlooked me,
when I packed everything into my Honda Civic Hatchback
and drove out of Oxford for the last time not because it was easy
but because it was the right thing to do.

The president and his faculty were irked but expelled no one,
too savvy about PR nightmares, and anyway, we would all
graduate soon enough, what did they care. They were old
enough to understand a year or two was nothing, waiting
us out—waiting anything out—was simpler in the scheme
of life, and now I think maybe the lesson was never
about rights and guts but that I did not matter
as much as I thought I did.

Before You Told Me

When I was a child in Ohio, surrounded by corn and soybean fields,
we used to run tornado drills in school. We hustled into hallways,
knelt down against walls. We covered our heads
with our innocent hands.

At a young age, I understood what to do: avoid windows,
find a place in the house, if no cellar or basement,
then at least the lowest floor, a bathroom with a tub,
a musty closet, a space below the stairs. I learned early on, too,
what to notice, how to predict: the sky a greenish tint,
the air swallowed into stillness.

I was just a little kid when a twister tore through the heart
of Xenia, eight miles away, ravishing homes
and lives in a path half a mile wide, the rubble reminding us
no one is safe, I could be next. Years later

I left Ohio to follow you to a state crowded with mountains
and an edge confronted by coast. I forgot about drills
I had grown up counting on. I forgot that
green might marinate the sky.

I forgot about silence:
its omens, its misfortunes.

Beginners

In the back of the refrigerator: this jar of seeds from so many
summers ago—our first? second?—when we bought pine planks
that became walls of raised bed. We hauled in a truckload of sand
so heavy when wet it could bury any good idea.
We tugged out a clean tarp then mixed compost—
manure, mushrooms—with soil dark enough to obscure
doubt and disappointment, things that we would swat at later
that season, that would chew on everything we grew. All those

harlequin bugs with their spots and persistence. They hid
below kale riddled with holes. The bugs swelled
and survived, and the plants yellowed yet lived on. The sun sugar
tomatoes broke open their orange bellies, still sweet despite brown
stems and speckled leaves. What was there to do but start over
the next year, and the next, and wait for pests and root rot
and blight? We twined tomatoes with copper. We sunk marigolds
into soil. We caught harlequin bugs by the handful,
knowing they'd already laid their eggs. How sure we were
we'd know better what to do through too hot or rainy seasons—
water less or water more. How sure, standing at the counter
every spring, that we had chosen better seeds.
How sure of our good fortune, that we had what we would need.

Katy Perry Is Crooning and Won't Stop Just Because I Did

Because this is a small village and people tell other people's news,
I already know when I walk past your mother's house
and the garage door is flung open wide
as if it got stopped mid-scream
and you are lining up the contents on the lawn
(an artificial Christmas tree, boards that once belonged
to shelves) that your brother died fifteen hours ago
in the early hours of morning, that he had trouble breathing
because of flu or because of some other condition the coroner
will discover—I will learn about that, too, surely, when the news
comes, because this is how a village runs: on private information,
on what really happened, on what maybe happened,
and especially if it's bad news, we pass it along like hot potatoes
so it won't burn our knowing hands, and in this way perhaps
it might not happen to us, not in the same way, or not so badly.

I pause at the edge of your lawn and pull out my earbuds—
Katy Perry is crooning and won't stop just because I did—
and tell you I heard about what happened and I'm sorry,
and you are startled because we have never talked
to one another but as happens in a small town, I know
who you are and you know who I am, by name anyway,
and you have forgotten for a moment the way a village runs:
on recognition and proximity. We must look each other
in the eye if we are to ever look at ourselves. You don't know
what crises I have lived through, for I moved away
and am only back now, and it isn't really fair
that I know about your brother today, and it isn't fair

that we are both alive and that his silver Grand Marquis sits
with a cold engine in the driveway and it isn't fair
that after I have expressed my sorrow for your loss
I can step back on the sidewalk and off your lawn.
I can slip the earbuds back in, and there will be Katy Perry,
still singing, and if I want her to start up again,
all I have to do is push rewind
which I won't
but I could

while you are left with the contents of the garage laid out on the lawn
and you won't be able to put any of it back
but you can't leave it out either
in the rain that is coming down already.

Tormenta de Tierra

A dirt storm marked by severe winds that carry dust, dirt, and sand. The storm develops in arid regions and often occurs during periods of drought.

The *tormenta* shrouds trees with soil.
With black teeth, the dirt storm eats Torreón.

Lights on Avenida Allende evanesce.
My *tía* cranks windows closed; howls
swipe the glass.

I shut the shelter of my room in her house.
Panes and wrought iron rattle from an anger exhumed,
spewing earth. Tonight

your call from Ohio
won't get through to me
in Mexico.

The phone and power lines
whip then snake on sidewalk.
By daybreak they'll lie still
but tangled.

Everything you hoped to say
gets stripped away like bits of blown trash
in this *tormenta de tierra.*
You'll try to thrash your way back
and make me change my mind about you,
about us.

Outside the safety of my *tía's* house,
soiled air billows like a black bridal veil
over street lamps and signs.

All night long, dirt drifts through the crack
below my door and silts the floor
like dust on a tomb.

In the morning,
I do not sweep it away.

Gold Rush

After the gold rush
a quiet in my middle states,
prairie grass fondling
the wind.

No one knows all that was filched
from the earth. Yellow dust
might still be worth something

if only we could catch it
with more than the tips
of our fingers.

After Dating the Man Who Told Me, "I Go to Places Too Dark for You"

I unravel the sweater
knit so tightly around my arms that when
the sleeves bare my wrists
I am surprised I still have hands.

On the Occasion of Our First
and Only Camping Trip, 1999

We'd been married one year that summer, the same season
Lance Armstrong won his first Tour de France, no revelation
yet of needles and scandals, of how a lie could look
like a harmless yellow band. Your friends asked us
to go camping. Months earlier, just before Valentine's Day,

the Senate acquitted Clinton, impeached no longer,
and it seemed as if things could take a turn that quickly:
become rotted then revived, start drowning but burst
above surface for air. We packed up sleeping bags
and a weather-beaten tent—we must have borrowed it,

for we did not own one then and never would—
but when night fell the temperature cascaded down
like leaves in autumn, their only resistance some useless
spin. The ground, rocky and cold, awaited as we argued over

who would sleep on the one inflatable mattress your friends
let us use. That summer everyone talked about what appliances
and machines and institutions would blow up or go kaput
in a few months when the year rolled into the new century.
But I was so young: what did I know of things

that could break based on expiration dates? In the end

we decided to share the two-inch mattress, two-feet wide.
I suppose we thought two was enough. The ground held us,
cold as indifference, and rocks burrowed into both our backs,
reminding us sharing means no one spares the other from pain.

I keep thinking Diana was still alive that summer, but no. By then
for two years she'd been dead.

What Mickey Wants

You're too young to wear a dress like that,
she tells me. She looks at me above
her lowered glasses.

Mickey doesn't think so. He's the one
who told me, Try it on.
You'd look hot in that,
he said, pointing to it
on the silver rack.

I'd yanked it
off the hanger, slid it onto my
pencil of a body and stared at the dodgy
dressing room mirror.

You still in there? she asks me.

Can he come back here
with me? I ask her.

Certainly not, she says. Instead,
she pulls aside the curtain and peers at me.
Oh, she says, Hm, is there another we
might like? You're too young

for that one.

I'm older than I look, I lie, Can I step out there
so he can see it?

Is that man your boyfriend?
(She points with a long and crooked finger.)

Sort of, I say.

She frowns. Go on then, she says,
waving me out.

Mickey is smoking, blowing rings
outside the shop's front door.
They float away into grey
unswaying sky.
I motion him inside,
and he crushes out his thin cigarette
with his dirty black boot.

When he pushes open the door,
the cold shoulders in.
Yep, just as I figured, he says,
Hot, real hot.

Really? I say.
But I'm glancing her way.
She stands, arms crossed,
lost in thought, looking out the window.
Hair piled high and pinned on top
of her head, like it might topple
over.

One day you'll be too old to be wearing
shit like that, he says, his eyes shifting
to her.

Trust me,
he says, Get it
while you can still

pull it off.

Escape

After a while, I knew
how to fold myself
into a thin line

like moth wings
pressed together
unlearning
how to fly.

I shed
pounds
of words
so what was left
whispered
in loose clothes.

Unnoticed,
and through the screen door,
I watched you
bunched on the concrete stoop
still belching out cuss words,
face engorged, roasted with rages
I could never anticipate,

the white plate—just shattered by you—
in shards like scattered teeth
still aching on linoleum,
no way for me to end this well.

All that time
I remained
tethered,
barely there,

just a strand
of long black hair

like the ones of mine you find
for months afterward
in your bed, on your clothes

everywhere.

If

If I were an avocado I could stop rot with the simple pit
of my heart. My seed would be celebrated, my scaly skin touched,
my worth determined by my tenderness.

I could stand against the acidity of your sliced tomatoes
and bite of jalapeño, and none of it would wither
who I was, who I might be. If I were an avocado

I could rise from where my mother once took root,
a land of saints and miracles, of water served in silver pitchers,
of siestas and serenades.

My name (no longer yours): *aguacate, palta*
butter fruit, alligator pear. I would cost more
than you would want to pay.

I would be neither savory nor sweet, and you could no longer
accuse me of extremes. I could remain on your cold shelf, tucked
beside the milk, butter, bread—behind the shut door of everything
you have forgotten—

and I would ripen.

All the Falafel Sandwiches We Ate in Paris

I slice and squeeze the thin-skinned lemon
and mince the garlic cloves into pieces as tiny
as truths best eaten slowly. I mash chickpeas
with a fork my mother gave us on our wedding day.
I add spoonfuls of tahini, and the thing necessary
to bring all flavors together: a dusting of salt.

When I taste the hummus, blended and smooth,
I remember all the falafel sandwiches we ate in Paris:
We waited in lines. We stood outside carryout windows. We counted
our money, which sometimes we had so little of. We wanted more.

We held the pita bread in our hands as if it were precious.
Indeed, this simple sandwich comprised everything we needed:
fried chickpea fritters, pickled cabbage, sliced onions, cucumbers,
eggplant, and, oh, that yogurt sauce we could not get enough of.
It seemed impossible to contain it all, so we gave up,

thinking it was easier that way: to let
what was so delicious
slip down our arms and drip
to the indifferent ground.

You Can Never Go Home Again

Here is a field, flailing with corn stalks blown by late-day winds.
Here is a highway leading in and out of towns you thought
you could forget: Byron, Clifton, Goes Station.
See how you didn't?

Here is the dairy farm that once sold homemade ice cream
and day-old doughnuts. There's a putt-putt course now
and a petting zoo and people sweating in line
for a Sunday hayride.

Instead of Grote's there's a Subway. Instead of stop signs
there's a stoplight. But there's your old school with its line
of wavy windows. Students still smoke on the corner,
lean against that fat stone someone spray-painted: the graffiti

of freedom. You thought you had it—and you did, didn't you?—
but you return, thirsty for streets you can name: Enon, Dayton,
Walnut. Everything you thought you could live without
so salty in your mouth.

The Day After Getting Back the Medical Test Results

If the one you love is curled up next to you
when you wake up, and you can feel each breath;
If you can hear the rumble of the train in the distance
and see the closet at the far end of the room, heavy
with sneakers and sweatshirts, and that scarf
your mother knitted for you that you do not wear
but cannot bear to give up because her hands
spent those hours on you;
If you can rise from your bed and walk on your own
to the bathroom, which you do a time or two each night,
and are doing now, in morning,
reaching for your husband's white terrycloth robe
because it's softer than your own;
If your dog has not piddled in the house overnight,
has held it in until you click open the door
and she flies out and toward cut grass, and if she
barrels toward you, afterward, as she always does,
a signal that you are someone's safety and sense of home;
If the sun falls into your front window
and the day promises to be long;
If you can taste the hazelnut in the coffee
and smell the mint plants as you water them,
the ones you put in the ground
yesterday in the late afternoon light;

If you know one person who loves you
for who you are—not the person you might be
but who you've become already—
and better yet, if you know more than one: the mother
who knitted you a scarf, the father who helps you
believe in a fair ever-after; the sister who tries to give
you what you want; the husband who holds you
when you worry

over the letter
that said
they want you
back in—

they need to know more.

Then it's more than enough to be grateful,
to focus on the sun and the spouse and the dog and the mint
and the grass and the gifts—all those gifts—
and the beginnings of the day,
not the ends. All those beginnings
beg you to believe—
they are enough,
and so you do.

Grand Theft

Those last two weeks we lived together—
when he turned the lock late
and sometimes not at all—
I could not sleep.

The world was disappearing: one dish, then four,
all the apple cider. The blender, pasta maker, the ice cream scoop,
and those rattling measuring spoons, held by a ring.
I imagined them clinking around
without me, scooping cumin and crushed coriander
for someone else.

Those green towels fled—the ones he used
to wipe away the last dashes of shaving cream—
and the bicycle out back, its broken kick stand,
and shelves of poetry books—with their thin spines
propping up a starving sort of love—
and then the shelves themselves
so the wall stood there naked
and shameless.

What remained? Everything difficult:
the rocking chair that creaked
the table with a crack
the furniture that wobbled.

I lay awake at night counting losses:
the wooden wind chimes that dangled
above the front porch stairs

and that one trip to Huatulco
now so long ago
when the truth
of how we felt
sounded in the shells.

I accused the walls of allowing all this thievery
then remembered I'd said—in the sand, in the slanted
light, in the early morning of our love—
what's mine is yours.

Inheritance

My great aunt was not the type of lady to smoke
out on the porch. No, she lit up in her living room, and up
and down the stairs, and in her bedroom on hot
Mississippi nights with the windows thrown open.

My great aunt read faster than other women cooked, cleaned,
baked cookies. One night she read *Gone with the Wind* cover
to cover while sitting on the toilet. She didn't have much use
for clocks or schedules: if she wanted to sleep, she slept.
She didn't have much use either for men who wanted to court her,
even if the man was her ex-husband, a Navy sailor who wanted
her back, a man she once loved. What did she need him for?
She had her own money from her government job after the war,
and then from when she started collecting vintage furniture.

She opened an antiques store on the first floor of her Vicksburg
hilltop house and sold enough not to have to bother
with customers who rang her doorbell when the day called
for a nap instead or when she had not yet drunk a cold bottle
of Coke or smoked her first cigarette of the day

or her last.

High cheekbones, big, almond-shaped, blue eyes—
my great aunt was the best kind of beauty: the kind who didn't care.

Her cantankerous calico cat, Miss Molly, slunk from me
and my sister. We were gentle girls and desperate to pet her.
The cat let no one near except my great aunt, who bought
Miss Molly cans of wet food and let her claw at whatever
antique chairs she pleased to scratch. My great aunt
made my father promise that when she died,
he would put down Miss Molly, too.

No one's going to take care of her the way I do.

My great aunt was long on conversation: sometimes
during our visits, we'd find our father in her kitchen
and hear her chattering in the living room.
We would ask him, *Who's she talking to?*
and he would answer:
Me.

But she was never short on opinions. If we went out to eat
her steak was always undercooked or overcooked, or the soup
too salty or too cold. She never hesitated
to send anything back. I was a young girl then.
I should have paid attention

for one day I would be given a thing or two
and not have the courage to send them back.

I was only seventeen when my great aunt Eloise
died. My father flew down to Mississippi
and took Miss Molly to the vet,
and into the casket the cat went.
                                                  I wonder about all
the other things my great aunt took with her,
things I'll never get back, answers to questions
I should have asked. I inherited the almond shape
of her eyes, though mine are brown, and an opal ring
she had crafted in Europe, a ring whose stone
eyes me with its bright specks and dazzle
and dares me to stand up straight
and have a damn opinion.

Puerto Escondido, Mexico

After breakfast, there is nothing to do
on the gritty streets where tourist
shops swell with halters, t-shirts, heat.

We walk the beach with its black streaks,
and blowfish and crab lie strewn
still damp, wide-eyed, bloated on sand.

It's a surfer's dream: waves chomping,
thrashing so hard I might lose
my suit in them. We pay for two plastic chairs

for the day, just today. Nothing to do
but watch the Dutch girl sunburn
and see surfers belly onto water

paddling toward horizon,
where there must be something for us
to do besides eat and wait and sleep

in a town of tequila specials
every off-season night. I find
a fat cockroach on the green tile

of the bathroom wall, and it skitters
from the light, from my shoe,
afraid of what I might do.

After She Calls and Says She Wants You Back

You're slicing up onions, making the whole kitchen cry,
even the cups I just washed, sweating on the drying rack,
no way to escape any mistakes you might make. You're cooking

for me again, this our fourth or fifth date, but you won't tell me
what you're preparing. A cast iron skillet you have owned
for much longer than we have known each other has a belly full

of olive oil rubbed into the places you have touched, saturated
with time and all your efforts. You take a garlic clove and crush
it with the flat of your knife and the heel of your hand: paper

wings spread open. The knife's wooden handle bears the outline
of your grasp. I think about the things you could take apart
with that blade: separate fat from meat, cut away the peel

to reveal the tender and sweet center. Chicken sizzles and sighs
in the skillet, and you leave it so long the skin burns just a little.
Still we will eat it, you and I, each of us hungry for something

we should not have.

Immigrant

you have to learn to live with emptiness
my mother told me   I drank water
when I was hungry   I drank water
the way people hustle onto trains rushing to another city

the rain begins in one window
but always finds its way to all the others

your dog scratches at the white couch I brought with me
the only thing left of mine I can still touch
in this place stuffed with dreams that stopped talking   long ago
we mistook the pelting of rain
and the refrigerator humming
and the sound of the mailman thunking our bills
into the box for our dreams still talking

your dog tears the fabric of my couch   the way lightning
rips open the belly of sky so you can't look at it without seeing
disaster

you call someone and they show up with a truck
hoist the couch out of the corner and into their arms and haul it out
the door I once entered   hungry   coins sewn into the stuffing
plunk to ground one by one and I think about what it means to

follow someone to the edge of nothing

the truck grumbles down our empty road   the rain answers

you have to learn

I sweep the wooden floor bereft of its face
I mop the place the couch covered like clothing
I wipe the fat baseboard with a rag wet with rain

I am so quiet now your breath has its own language
I still don't understand

Beso, Beso

This is for the red cup you filled and and handed me,
how you followed me to the kitchen, crowded with someone else's
sink and stove and set of spoons, a room filled with things
we both wanted some day: stacks of plates that promised meals,
silver hooks for warm towels to sop up messes, pots
with lids that did not match but kept water from boiling over.

This is for the little piece of paper
with my name and number, a wasp of a thing with its sting,
so easy to fly away. You held on, unafraid.

This is for the blue bedspread underneath the elm,
the steaming potstickers we picked up
with forks instead of chopsticks—we learned so much
later how to grasp with more tender weapons—
and for the bike you leaned against the side of my car
without scarring it the first time you spent the night.

This is for the plastic radio you brought over, kept on, which cast out
bad news and country tunes, a radio that always drained new batteries.
This is for the scratching of squirrels up and down the walls, squirrels
we never caught, and for the hard rain that soaked through the roof
two nights in a row, when you slept with a fist at your ear.
This is for the hammer and set of wrenches you kept
in a yellow toolbox, and for the birdhouse you built me
where chickadees twisted nests with pieces of yesterday's mail.

And the backyard we borrowed, the wisps of smoke
and smell of sticks and paper on fire, and the buttered corn
you made me hold in foil over flames. This is for that fight
we had, stitched with grey wool from your winter coat,
the one you kept buttoning back up. You were telling me
you were leaving, letting in the draft of December by opening my door
but not shutting it. You stayed one more year, then two: they
were cooked with sautéed okra, salt, chicken skin. We warmed
our hands over the stove when the heat went out. We slept
with our shoes on. We listened to the twitching light bulb
in the next room, too weak to remain on, too strong to darken.

This is for the clinking of glass—*beso, beso*—
at my cousin's wedding, and how you got drunk later and yelled
at the taxi driver for taking the long and fragmented way
back to the hotel we had chosen but could not afford, its pool by then
covered by canvas. The leaves whirled like pinwheels
in the park we passed, the swings swaying,
emptied of children.

This is for that morning a year later when you showed up at the lake—
a body of water, wide-mouthed, yawning. Trees trembled,
fragile in their reflection. You waited for me to wake up
and follow you anywhere, for the light to stumble on
as it always had. This is for that light, what it can bear,
how it can falter through a clear window.
Then the jangling of the green truck
in which you drove away, the last time, a pipe or fender
or all of it come loose, the sound like janitor's keys
hanging from a ring,
so many doors to open
yet none of them home.

Perhaps It Is Useless to Tell You Now

that I still remember
the long drive to Indiana to see your parents,

the way the highway became a seam
down the fabric of your life before and after me.

Out of morning fog, their grey barn emerged,
one window's glass cracked like a cobweb.

An animal scrabbled around the attic
above the bedroom where I stayed

and in the morning your mother fried eggs
that your father poked with a fork and said were too cold.

The dog broke loose one afternoon
and your father sent us out to find him

and we were young enough then to think it was easy
to bring anything back and we drove miles down country lanes

winding past creeks and weeping willows
over bridges that made us bump in our seats

until we tracked him down, wet and panting,
his fur muddy yet warm.

It was summer after all, and the light cared less that season
how late and long anyone stayed out. It woke us early anyway.

Your parents kept a picture on the mantle of the last girl
you loved, and she smiled at the lot of us

as your father flipped channels, landing on Wheel of Fortune.
I wonder now if luck had anything to do with us

if we had more or less or none at all
but thought we did, how long such a belief sustained us.

We ate chocolate ice cream after your father went to bed.
You held the spoon under hot water. You washed

the yellow bowl afterward and put it away
so no one would know.

You hung your mother's dishrag,
grey and limp, on its hook.

I never returned to Indiana, never smelled
the split-open crabapples fallen on the autumn floor

never heard the ice crack in the pond behind the house that winter
never witnessed the white seeds of dandelions

escape their stems in spring.
By then I was in Mexico, already forgetting

how you stole into my room in your father's house,
or I stole into yours, how there was a time when rules
would not keep us apart.

Cooking

I used to know how to toss things
in a skillet, how to crumble leftovers
together and make a decent meal.

Now I only follow recipes,
go down the list of ingredients,
check them all off. There are rules to know,
rules I once ignored.

A single ingredient before another,
only this much of that one thing—
minced ginger, tablespoon of curry,
quarter cup of scallions—
or it might ruin the dish, throw
all the flavors off,
make a mess of the intended taste.

I used to date boys who bent rules,
who said things they did not mean,
or did things they wanted to retrieve
later with mouthfuls of apologies.

They broke up and came back
but it was hard to tell after a while
if they were coming or going,
if it was the first time or the last.

I dated men with no jobs
but with professed ambitions; men with demands
about how I spent my Sunday evenings.
Men who flirted hard
but not always with me.

They broke rules, but I broke them, too.
I re-dated men. I dated men with cats,
men separated but not yet divorced,
men who held Bibles too tightly
in their hands. Men with tempers.
Men who loved their mothers
but did not like them.

I went from winging it—thrashing for
sweet when all was bitter—

to going back to the list:
kind, honest,
makes me laugh.
Blends into my family.
Lets me speak.
Says what he means.

And then the rules:
Take one big trip before committing.
Watch how he talks about his last love.
Don't skip steps. Don't accept substitutions.
Remember a simmer works better than a boil.
If it burns, toss it out, start all over.
Don't try to save something
already losing
all its flavor.

Designed by Fire

From the NC Botanical Garden on its Coastal Plain and Sandhills Habitats: "This natural habitat garden is burned yearly to stimulate processes which are part of the endangered longleaf pine ecosystem. Fire plays an important part in promoting the growth of a high diversity of plants here and in the real pine savannas of the state."

We stand still before the pine savanna.

From this once-ignited tract,
pitcher plants, butterwort and sundew
spring up in the clearing they tag,
"designed by fire." Pine cones release seed,
making new from flame.

Earlier, we sat on rock
over Meeting-of-the-Waters Creek.
Our feet dangled
but never touched the cool
below as we talked about our future,
what can grow in this space
where our failed marriages have cracked
and sizzled our courage and beliefs.

We flung words—*I don't know if*
and *we might never*
be able to—
like smoldering brush
at each other

and they stung.

And now, where I could only see our blackened spirits,
there is this: the small pine trees waving back and forth,

defying me.

This Way Home

A few feet from the road: a deer on its side, legs stiff
and sticking out as if someone had tipped it over
with one nudge when it should have taken a calamity
to barrel it down. All it took was one person's rushed journey,
cut short by something you never saw coming.

I know this way home to Ohio, out of Tennessee
and taking 23 on the Eastern side of Kentucky,
the highway like a crack up and down the state.

There's another, on the berm, white puff of tail. How long ago?
This morning? Last night? That's two if you are counting,
which I am not.

I drive in and out of Pikeville, Prestonsburg, Paintsville,
all these places not far from where my father kicked stones
as a boy, stuck his head between the stairs, lit the lawn
on fire instead of mowing it, almost blazed the house, too.
Such wild and daring youth.

I pass yellow, fallow fields.

Another, and another, rigor mortis long set in. That's four
if you are counting, which I tell myself not to do. It's pointless
to add up the things that will outnumber me. Towns
with shuttered windows squint at me as I travel through.
A train rattles along, pulling rusted cars, paralleling
this highway that is at once too long
and never long enough.

My father calls, asking where I am, what mile. I'm not
exactly lost, just not keeping track of my location. I'm
at a rest area, I tell him. The wind is picking up leaves
and scattering them the way we do
so many of our days.

Grey clouds growl.

Another deer, knocked over, hoofs off the ground. Five if I were—
but I am not. Cities rise and fall in front of, behind me. For rent,
for lease, for sale, what in heaven's name doesn't
diminish in value?

I'm almost there, I want to tell my father,
who is no longer on the phone.

Rain quenches my journey's thirst.

A sixth deer, dead on the side of the road, if any of us are counting,
which we all eventually do. I press the accelerator
as one does luck—

hard if you are willing.

Secret Ingredient

When I want to please my father, I cook butternut squash.
Peel and boil, broth and curry, mash the soft squash
against the sides of the silver pot that for two decades
has managed magic: solids to liquids, disparate
to inextricably together.

When I want to comfort my mother, I bake fudgey cake
from a tattered recipe that calls for cups of chocolate chips,
pecan halves, cocoa powder. Glaze slips down the sides,
solidifies when cool. My mother shaves off slivers,
licks the knife clean.

When I want to feed my sister, it's white bean soup:
great northern, grown in the Midwest, just like we were,
where one summer she painted the picket fence, and I cooked
us two frozen dinners: Salisbury steaks, gravy, potatoes,
apple pie. Cicadas rattled songs from trees after seventeen
years. The sun hung onto the early evening sky,
the light of youth and never enough. We ate sitting
cross-legged on the grass, scraping the bottom
of our tin trays.

For my husband, it's red lentils with cayenne pepper,
a squeeze of lime, chopped cilantro. When we've run out
of words, I add a dollop of sour cream, and it melts
into the dish without needing answers. When he's tired,
when he's down, I bake a yogurt custard pie with berries,
a crust crushed from ginger snaps and strawberry jam.
It's a dessert of opposites: baked then chilled, sweet yet tart,
the outside cracked, the inside soft.

When I miss the once, the used to be, I soak black beans
overnight as stars slip across the Southern sky.
In the morning, I add bay leaves, more than necessary.
My mother used to make it look so easy: chopped onions,
minced garlic, cumin and coriander and a long boil. It is simple
but takes some time. Toward the end, I shred tortillas, crack
open eggs and drop them in, wait until the yolks cloud over,
a pan of yellow eyes going blind.

Lost in Tennessee

When you don't know who you are,
go outside. Look up

through the branches of big trees—maple, sweet gum, poplar.
The leaves know how to drink the light, how to use it to live,
how to throw shadows on the ground. Listen

to the birds—brown thrasher and white-throated sparrow.
They know when to sing; they know when silence matters.

Touch the grass—tall fescue or zoysia, makes no difference.
It knows how to grow
after each cut.

Watch the weeds in the field—black medic and wild carrot.
They know how to take over
they know not to take no for an answer
they know to bloom anyway.

Fast Love

In your damp basement
apartment, in your living room
with one chair, years before the divorce,
long before we met up outside a bookstore
to exchange flickering lamps and a nicked table
and one deed, way before we slept on the east coast
and west coast of our bed, before we spent a week
apart and did not phone, before you went out with the boys
and I caught the late bus after work, before we ate falafel
sandwiches on Paris streets and let the sun tell us how long
the days would last, before we sanded the oak table we bought
with what little money we had, before we moved to a state
where neither of our families lived to remind us we were loved,
before we held hands under the maple and I wore white and you
black and leaves clung to summer, before we ambled the cobbled
paths of Taxco and slept against each other on a bus to Oaxaca,
before you stirred my tea in your cup in your damp
basement apartment, before we really
knew each other

did we ever really know each other?

in your living room with one chair, you flicked on your stereo
and George Michael sang while we danced
and the room did not seem damp
or small
or underground.

We had wings then

didn't we?

We had sky.

Binding

This little line
is a twine of rope,
a coil to swing

down to you. Not like a
noose, but a string
of yarn to knit us

together. This verse is for us
tonight, on different streets
paved with a glaze

of rain. This is for you,
dear, for our quiet
unhappiness that tangles

like a silver web:
sticky, and thin as thread.

After the Diagnosis

I stopped planting annuals—no more petunias
or geraniums or zinnias I longed to have come back
without my bidding. I planted Lenten roses, daffodils,
daylilies whose color I forgot so they would surprise me
in summer: orange persimmon, showlight, mystic amulet,
wispy morn. I put in the ground every kind of sedum I could
find—dynomite, rosy glow, dragon's blood. Year after year,
through a drought and too much rain they struggled but rose
from the earth—despite neglect, late frosts and later snow—
with stems as strong as legs, and roots that burrowed deep
into the ancestry of the soil. And now it is late March,
and every bulb I ever planted pushes up, nudges toward
tomorrow, and all that sedum I planted years ago—
on my hands and knees, dirt beneath my
nails—obeys the sun's command
and grows.

An Unexpected Visitor

When you arrived, I heard the clacking of the stacking of stones, one against the other; the shoveling of dirt, the spade digging and tossing aside. When you snuck in, the dust lingered on my fingertips. Your rain robbed me of peace, wet rhythms against my windows, and when it stopped, the shadow of the sun grew long but also short again, the black puddle it made a mere dot if I waited until noon, if I held my breath. When you left, I heard things differently: the creak on the stairs sounded less despair than surprise. The sky sighed, the whistle of the trees calling back the wind. The seasons shifted one to the next, sweet and damp. The grass felt slick after rain, and honesty and truth felt soft, like fur or velour or anything from my childhood when the future was a word without sticks and matches. I sang, too, filling my lungs with bigger gulps of dreams. Birds warbled stories of worm and birth. The air turned from crisp to warm to sticky, and the salt on my skin reminded me I was of this earth, to trust and not stare at my feet. I looked up and saw the tops of reaching trees, and firelight in sunrise. The clouds took their time, abandoning their needs. If you come back, which you could, which you might not ever, but if you do, tread softly through the door and into the heart of my house. Do not wake the others. Gently, just touch me.

What a Poem Wants

No longer than fourteen lines,
it stitches metaphors down its seams.
It gleams with ink-streams
of mundane, yet hopes for the divine.

It breaks its rhythmic fences.
Words wander—such restless,
unkempt animals.

It yearns to trim its weight,
pluck out parasitic words,
loosen its maiden stay.

It longs to wash down the page,
a desert's thirsty rain

and to be two-faced, double-edged,
to live infinite lives.

On Sundays

So many years it took to master
those Sunday lessons taught in my *tía's* tiny kitchen—
not the way to break open the bellies of *bolillo*
and spread butter and beans onto bread,
not how to make *caldo* with chicken bones
and *calabacita* and *cebolla* we had selected
and weighed with a cast iron scale
at the little garage market blocks away.

What I'm telling you is on those Sundays
when my *primas* gathered in my *tía's* kitchen—
while their husbands and children kicked
soccer balls outside the screen door—
when Lalin stirred whatever soup steamed on the stove,
when Fanro dunked her hands, her whole arms
into the sink and scrubbed knives and pans
and cutting boards, when Ati squeezed
thin-skinned *limones* and let the juice run free
into my *tía's* old aluminum pot
while I scraped the papaya clean
of black seeds, I often wondered why the women
got stuck with all that Sunday work.

Oh so many things I did not know.

In my *tía*'s crowded kitchen, my *primas* talked with
and over each other so that you had to have pluck
to finish a sentence before it drifted into the next. Their
words mingled and their voices and laughter rose
and fell, but mostly rose like the swirl
of incense, like a kind of
fervent prayer

that came to me only years later
in my own place of sanctitude
where no one could tell me
whatsoever the things
that I should do.

Savior

Your hands pop open the hood of the car,
drain the oil, twist the cap shut, stop the leak.

Your hands pump the colander and wash
shaking leaves clean.

Your hands cut the sunflowers, brown and yellow heads
already drooping from the long drive you must make
to see me through this terrible heat,
the kind that causes rashes, that beats
down on back doors. Your hands

used to know how to take off things
in the late afternoons, when we shoved
our books aside and slept on deadlines,
when I thought the world was made for straps
and sundresses without destinations.

Your hands used to know how to stop me from going.
They used to tell me a story. Now, they break up
a sentence into small pieces. They clear clutter.

They're strong enough to pull someone from a burning car,
just not your car, just not me.

Acknowledgments

I started this book in my twenties, when I was a wide-eyed undergraduate student at Wittenberg University and studying poetry with Imogene Bolls. She's the one who introduced me to poets like Mary Oliver. Professor Bolls and I used to sit in her office and talk about poetry, and though her office was small and dark, there was light there for me, and openness. During that time, I was also editor of the college literary magazine, and Professor Bolls was the magazine's faculty advisor. There was a crisis of sorts (it's hard now through the lens of decades to call a problem with a college lit mag a "crisis," though it sure felt like it back then), and Professor Bolls stuck by me and my decisions without hesitation. I will always be grateful to her.

I intended to do an MFA in poetry right after I graduated from Wittenberg, but I didn't, and instead I ended up in a master's degree program in journalism at The Ohio State University. (What? Journalism? That's a long story I won't tell here.) One year into the two-year program, I decided to quit (the program was solid and good, but it wasn't my passion—my heart was in poetry). Then my dad called me up and told me, "You're already halfway through. You'll never regret having a master's degree." I decided to stay, but I knew the only way to get through the program was to fill up my electives with creative writing courses. I applied to get into a graduate-level poetry class, but the professor of that class told me she wasn't going to let me in, that my poems were too sentimental. I didn't give up, though, and applied to get into David Citino's graduate-level poetry class instead. He let me in—thank goodness—and gently and patiently taught me what was sentimental and how to change it, if I wanted. I took more than one class with him my second year, and I am not exaggerating when I say those classes got me through my journalism program. I never did regret the master's degree, and it did positively impact my entire career, but it's my love of poetry that has sustained me through moves, heartbreak, loneliness, and the swerves of life.

Professor Bolls and Professor Citino are no longer alive, but I still want to thank them first and foremost. They both pushed me to be a better writer, and their teachings gave me a solid foundation in poetry, as well as in kindness and humanity. Their lessons live on in my work and in my life.

I also want to thank:

—Don Wallis, who took a bunch of us didn't-know-what-we-were-doing teens and allowed us to write poetry and believe in ourselves.

—All of the people in my writing groups over the years who have read my work and given me feedback. A special shout-out to Corinne Mahoney, Allen Huff, and Pat Locke.

—My MFA from Queens University. Though I did not focus on poetry when I finally got my MFA, I certainly became a much better writer because of the program.

—All the editors of literary magazines and journals who accepted my poems. It's always a good day when an acceptance comes in, and I know how hard these editors work. An especially big thank you.

—My writer friends who are in the trenches with me every day.

—All the people and experiences who inspired poems. Please remember, however, that poems do not have to be based on truth and facts! My imagination has always been my constant companion.

—My dear family, including my husband, Preston McKee; my parents, Hap and Sonia Cawood; and my sister, Romy Cawood. My father and sister are both poets themselves, and I am grateful for my genes.

—The judge who selected my book for the Adrienne Bond Award in Poetry, for valuing my work.

—Emily Fine, who talked me into submitting my manuscript for this contest.

—Marc Jolley and Mercer University Press, for working with me to make a long-ago dream come true. Ever since I was a teenager, I always imagined my first book would be a poetry collection. Although it didn't turn out that way, I am beyond thrilled to finally see the poems I have been carving and chiseling for decades finally go out into the world, together.